Introduction

The Teacher's Little Instruction Book was written *for* teachers *by* teachers, with over a half century of classroom experience and wisdom.

Each page contains suggestions, inspirational quotes, advice, practical application, creative insights and time-tested ideas that relate to the awesome privilege and responsibility of teaching.

Easy to take along and easy to read — for instant inspiration. This little book is packed with all the motivation and encouragement you could ever hope to find.

If you've ever wanted to touch a life and teach a child the art of living, then this book was designed for you!

It's like getting your whole desk pples!

Acknowledgements

A special note of appreciation is extended to Michael T. Johnson, for his valuable assistance on this project.

The most valuable gift you can give another is a good example.

5

Keep all promises you make
(or have a good explanation for not doing so)!

The capacity to inspire is one of the teacher's greatest offerings.

6

Let your students know your hopes, goals, and aspirations for them —
individually and in group settings.

Children are very concerned with what is fair.

7

Remember due process.

Hear both sides of the story, even if you witnessed the incident.

Model courtesy, good manners, and sportsmanship.

Students are like mirrors. They reflect
our attitudes in life.

Encourage a sense of responsibility.

Challenge your students
to experience this by
helping them choose and
accomplish service projects
for their school and community.

9

Break monotonous routines

10

An opened window with a fresh breeze, or modified lighting, can perk things up.

Be genuine.

11

Be willing to say
"I don't know,"
but not too often.

You are a role model, even if at times, you wish you were not.

12

Practice apologizing on occasion. It may be
the first time some students
have heard this done with grace and dignity.

Learn how to spin a good story.

13

Telling a good story
can develop within your students a
hunger to know more.

Don't let any Report Card grade be a surprise, to either parents or students.

14

Make introductory phone calls to parents at the beginning of the year. If they get to know you on a friendly basis, tough calls at a later time will be easier.

Be prepared for the unexpected.

15

A great tool to keep in your desk
is a well-stocked first-aid kit.

In a parent-teacher conference, rather than offering your opinion, simply state the facts objectively.

16

In discussing a child's problems, describe the behavior and let the parents draw the conclusion.

The test of good manners is being able to put up with the bad ones.

— Maurice Seitler

17

Set the example for students. Use phrases such as "Thank you," "Please," and "I appreciate that."

The best preparation for tomorrow is the right use of today.

18

"PLAN A" might not work.
Prepare "PLAN B" in advance.

Reading is to the mind what exercise is to the body.

19

Teach students the fun of reading. Read aloud to them from captivating stories. At the end, have them read aloud so they discover the outcome for themselves!

One of the most important
roles of the teacher
is that of encourager.

20

Let your students know you believe in them.
Praise publicly. Reprimand privately.

Failure isn't fatal.

Students simply need
someone who cares enough
to help them get beyond the hurdle.

A student can be happy all week because of one good compliment.

— Adapted from Mark Twain

22

Individually and openly acknowledge
the gifts, talents, and positive traits
you observe in your students.

Healthy and effective teachers take time to nurture themselves, too.

23

After a frustrating day, give yourself a break!
Change your routine that evening.
Treat yourself to something you enjoy.

The teacher is the preserver of civilization.

24

Take your students the way they come to you — not the way you wish they were. Then, help them improve.

The teacher is the guardian of the nation's treasure — its children.

25

Develop a vision for your students.
When you look at them, see beyond the obvious.

If you respect your profession, others will respect it — *and you, too!*

Affirm your profession.
Think positively. Speak optimistically.

26

Appropriate the sailor's prayer: "Oh Lord, Your sea is so great and my boat is so small."

27

When the load seems heavy, remind yourself out loud: "I have summers free!"

With a difficult child, affirm to yourself: "This child is going to make it!"

28

Make the worthwhile investment.
Spend a little extra time with the child
who makes life difficult for you.

One of your most important achievements is to teach respect.

Model respect for your students.

Make a point to learn something from your students each day.

29

Courtesy and kindness are hard to give away. They are known to come back home again.

30

Express to students that their care and safety are important to you.

Curiosity is a valuable trait to encourage.

31

Teach a curiosity for understanding and
appreciating the environment.
Inspire the desire to protect it.

Document, document, document!

A "behavior book" is a good idea in which children must sign their names when they misbehave. This is both good reinforcement and documentation.

A teacher's warnings, admonitions, and reprimands must suitably fit the student's misconduct.

33

Keep a tape recorder on your desk. A recording of a child's verbal misconduct for later evaluation with parents, speaks for itself!

34

Wise teachers protect themselves.

Carry liability insurance.

Wise teachers exercise healthy boundaries.

35

Never work alone with a child and avoid having children ride in your car with you.

Communicate, communicate, communicate!

36

Make your Principal aware of a behavioral
problem prior to his or her hearing
from angry parents.

Avoid the expression that life was much tougher when you were their age.

37

Show compassion for the problems and concerns your students face today.

The smile on your face is the light in the window that tells students you are home.

38

Tune into your students' creativity and intelligence by smiling at them as you listen to their questions and ideas.

Children who are cruel to others need suitable discipline.

39

Defend the child who is
being picked on.
Deal directly with cruel
behaviors. Deal specifically with
unpleasant attitudes.

Being rudely interrupted is annoying.

40

Practice the same manners you expect
of your students.
Refrain from rudely interrupting them.

Teachers should encourage empathy in their students by modeling it.

41

When a child is hurt by another, model genuine concern for the wounded child.

Children love to feel
accepted for themselves
and praised for their own
unique qualities.

42

Ignore the issue of racial differences unless
racism raises its ugly head.

Then move swiftly and boldly to confront it.

Never leave your classroom unsupervised.

43

Make friends with a buddy teacher and take
turns so you can step away when needed.

Stay involved.

44

Find out about activities
important to your students.
Attend when you can.
Your support will build bridges to
your students' hearts.

Teachers should share their sense of humor with their students.

45

When the end of the year comes and your students chant, "No more school! No more books!" — sound your own comparable rhyme!

Comparing a student to his outstanding sibling is always a major no-no.

46

Appreciate the unique qualities which lie within your student. Acknowledge his or her creativity as a valuable talent in itself, not necessarily correlating with intelligence, grades, or degrees.

Rise above pettiness.

47

Nurturing slights and cruel words will create
bitterness between you and your students.

Reward hard work and accomplishment by integrating fun and activities into the day.

Provide time for table games. Encourage students to learn the rules and to play by them.

If each person would sweep in front of his own door, the whole world would soon be clean.

49

Encourage students to develop good habits of cleanliness and orderliness.

Encourage good hygiene while refraining from pointing out a particular child.

Encourage accountability.

The task you most want to postpone is the one you ought to do first.

50

A notebook is a great place to catch
your flashes of brilliance and creativity —
for jotting down your ideas and those things
you need to do.

A smile adds a great deal to face value.

Remember, you are the key to the environment in your classroom.

Celebrate with your students!

Openly acknowledge the accomplishments of your students. Remember their birthdays. It costs so little and means so much.

Your pleasantness and optimism, especially on tough days, are appreciated and respected by your students.

53

Wear a happy face. Ask a question, then calmly and patiently give your students time to think before you require an answer.

Set an example for appropriate conduct in word and deed.

54

Don't repeat rumors. Never use a word which, when quoted back to you, would cause you embarrassment. Practice being good-natured, flexible, and willing to compromise.

Tell me, and I'll forget. Show me, and I may remember. Involve me, and I will understand.

— Chinese proverb

55

Involve students in role-playing to let them experience taking responsibility for themselves rather than taking the easy way out — through blame.

Modeling a strong work ethic turns your labor into an opportunity for teaching.

56

Let the students see that not everything is easy for you. Let them see that you, as well as they, have to put effort into assignments.

An effective teacher plans, organizes, and keeps one step ahead.

57

Arrive at least five minutes early to work. Preview videos and filmstrips before showing. Label all property and instructional materials, as well as the date purchased. Take good care of those things you borrow and return them on time.

That which is learned with pleasure is learned in full measure.

58

Treat the student's mind as more than a
muscle or a bucket into which
you pour knowledge.

Model morality and ethics.

Integrate what moral and
ethical values you can
legally present into your
teaching.

59

Friendship is a plant that one must water often.

60

Occasionally sit with your students at lunch.
Develop a system where deserving students are
rewarded by "having a soft drink with the
teacher." Use these times to get valuable
feedback from your students. Be prepared
to take the bad with the good.

Swallowing angry words is much better than having to eat them.

61

Even when you are in the right, never use the word "liar." Instead say, "The facts have been improperly stated."

The best way to forget your own problem is to help someone else solve theirs.

Help your students understand and control
their tender and confusing emotions — anger,
sadness, jealousy, and envy
would be good places to start.

Each new day affords the opportunity to help students believe in themselves.

63

Always label students' questions as important — having significance and meaning.

64

Readers are leaders.

Reinforce, often, the value and
fun of reading books!

Stories from the history of teaching can offer the contemporary teacher priceless perspective.

65

Read the following books: *The Hoosier Schoolmaster*, *The Thread That Runs So True*, and *Christy*. Observe how the teaching profession has changed and how it has not. Make notes of those values and principles from yesterday which you would like to bring into your classroom today.

I wondered why someone
didn't do something.
Then I realized that I was
"someone."

Be responsible.

Be prompt when stern duty calls.

The best preparation for tomorrow is the proper use of today.

67

Plan for presenting materials several different ways to accommodate the various learning styles among your students.

An astute teacher keeps good records.

68

Keep track of expenditures for your class. Save
receipts, and take tax credit. Keep current
records of all staff development. Prepare a
form with appropriate biographical information
for parents to complete for their children.

Students don't care how much you know until they know how much you care.

69

Always pay attention to warning signs of possible abuse or suicide.

The heart is the happiest when it beats for others.

70

Help a new student get connected with the established "group." You can do this by assigning team projects, reassigning seating, or establishing a rotating buddy system among your students.

Discerning teachers demonstrate respect for their colleagues.

71

Refrain from speaking disapproval toward colleagues,
in the classroom or otherwise, which is certain to get
back to them. Demonstrate interest
in the special events of your colleagues' lives.

I guard my words with care,
and keep them soft and sweet.
I never know, you see,
which ones I'll have to eat.

If you say something you shouldn't, apologize quickly.
Promptly inform the Principal or your Supervisor.

72

In a parent conference, begin with a compliment toward the child, end with a compliment toward the child, and sandwich the difficult news in between.

73

Practice optimism.

See the glass as half full rather than half empty.

The voice of the world speaks to you in the tone of your own voice.

74

Think twice before speaking.
Your words, good or bad, encouraging or
critical, could be remembered
for a lifetime.

A gracious teacher uses impulse control.

75

Always answer an unpleasant letter after anger has passed. Discuss pertinent issues only. When confronted with a grievance, disarm tension by showing your willingness to cooperate. Use positive affirmation while solving the problem.

An enlightened teacher responds rather than reacts.

76

To strengthen your own position, handle as many discipline problems yourself as you can. However, when confronted with abusive language and/or behavior, calmly leave the scene. Seek the Principal's counsel.

Some people have greatness thrust upon them. Very few have excellence thrust upon them — they achieve it.

77

— John Gardner

To achieve happiness, do creative, excellent, wholesome things. Happiness will naturally follow.

The most important part of your plan will be the task of following through.

78

Follow through is more important than *planning for*. Practice the cardinal virtue — self-discipline.

Trying to achieve success by aiming to please everyone is a sure formula for frustration.

79

You will never please everyone,
but a great sense of accomplishment comes
when a good compromise can be made.
This applies to both students and parents.

Organize, organize, organize!

Organization brings peace. Collect neat boxes
and containers specifically for those
miscellaneous items you want accessible
on a moment's notice.

A meeting is where minutes are kept and hours are lost.

81

In meetings and conferences, be certain not to waste the time of others. In the classroom, try to allot enough time for students to work on their assignments, giving enough time for questions or clarification before class ends.

All people smile in the same language.

Remember, you don't get
two chances
to make a good first impression.

Turn every situation, even potentially unpleasant ones, into a pleasant learning experience.

83

Don't let a situation of tension between students go unresolved. Encourage and teach people skills. Give them specific examples of how this could help them be more successful as an "adult" (key word!). Walk them through the steps of resolution. After all is settled, be sure to follow up with your appreciation to both parties.

When appropriate, let your students be involved in the planning and decision making.

84

They will feel connected and involved. Emphasize the fact that democracy includes both majority rule and a concern for the rights of the minority.

A degree or two, with your teacher education included, will provide a good *start* for you in the teaching profession.

85

Your real education occurs in the classroom.

To create and sustain interest, the dynamic teacher incorporates anecdotes and illustrations into the learning process.

86

Consider telling a funny story at the end of the day as a reward for good behavior.

Students love novelty.

87

In the upper grades, consider including a
nonsense question in each test, such as:
"Who is buried in Grant's tomb?"

Balance learning with fun!

88

Utilize community resources, such as
the Historical Society, a public art festival,
museums or the city zoo.

Try reviewing for tests in the format of a game.

89

Students respond to a teacher's sense of fun, which can make learning more agreeable, pleasant, and most important, memorable!

The best teachers are sensitive in human relations.

90

Creatively decorate your hallway and classroom. Involve your class! For example: collecting leaves in the Fall.

Put energy and imagination into your everyday tasks!

91

Holidays and the change of seasons are more
exciting for students when you involve them
in seasonal programs, displays
and activities.

Ideas are funny little things! They won't work unless you do.

— Stan Toler

92

Express only those promises
you can live up to.

Always dress professionally.

93

You will rarely be criticized for looking too dressed up.

94

Give yourself a break!

Time at home should include
periods of no schoolwork.

Be open to learning from others.

95

Receive counsel from an experienced teacher, creative insight from a younger teacher, or inspiration from a gifted or special student!!

Never lose touch with your sense of purpose.

96

Teachers want to be successful because of personal and professional pride — but mainly because they want to see their students succeed.

Stay up-to-date.

97

Well-rounded teachers incorporate significant
current events into their teaching. Read
newspapers and magazines. This will help in
class discussion.

Part of the educational task must be that of teaching students life skills.

98

Develop safety consciousness within your students. Prepare them for fire, tornado drills, CPR and other lifesaving possibilities.

Professionalism is an important part of a good teacher's mind-set.

99

Politely decline to discuss a child's problems at the supermarket or mall. Invite the parent to make an appointment.

The study of geography and our natural resources is an important part of the learning process.

100

Keep maps readily available. Encourage reports on vacations which cover natural sites. Invite photos to be discussed and posted from summer trips and excursions.

He who dares to teach should never cease to learn.

101

Become a lifelong learner. Stay fresh and vibrant by learning something new every day.

102

When I am wrong, dear Lord, make me easy to change, and when I am right, make me easy to live with.

— Peter Marshall

If you are too big for criticism,
you are too small for praise.

Getting off to the right start can set a positive tone for the rest of the year.

Join the parent-teacher organization promptly each year. Let the students share in the development of the classroom rules.

Discover your own genius!

104

Regarding teaching methods and style, you must work out your own formula. Know yourself, develop your techniques around your own strengths. You will enjoy the journey so much more!

Be equipped for handling student disagreements.

105

Set a place and meeting time between the
students where they can peacefully talk out their
differences. Do it privately, where they can speak
openly without embarrassment or teasing
from their peers.

Keep your face to the sunshine and you cannot see the shadow.

— Helen Keller

106

In a problem, an appeal to the child's sense
of sportsmanship may succeed
when nothing else will.

No one is useless in the world who lightens the burden of it for anyone else.

— Charles Dickens

107

Teach your students to leave their mark. Pick a service project which touches the heart of your students. Consider ground's beautification, donations to charity or a local food bank, or planting a garden to attract birds or butterflies.

There are two sides to every argument — until you decide to take one.

108

When you have recurring problems with a student, and the student's parents say you are the only teacher with whom their child has had a problem, check with his or her previous teacher. This will give you a wider scope of the facts and offer insight for dealing with a specific personality type from the wisdom of one who has been there.

The larger the island of knowledge, the longer the shoreline of wonder.

— Ralph W. Sockman

109

Go through your materials every three years, at least. This will keep information, especially visuals, appropriately current.

Students appreciate being kept informed.

110

Initiate a chart of school events, team awards, due dates for important assignments or for *outstanding* behavior! Students will visit the chart often to check things out!

Courage is fear that has said its prayers.

— Harle Wilson Baker

111

Keep a notebook of ideas with handy ways to challenge bright students and brighten challenging students. Add to it as the years go by. Keep tabs of successful results for future reference and that occasional needed stroke.

Keep a tidy classroom.

112

A cluttered room is not conducive to good learning.

Class is courtesy in word, attitude, and action.

113

Send thank-you notes promptly for gifts and
thoughtful gestures from parents, and students,
as well as community volunteers
who give of their time.

Part of the learning process is teaching students character.

114

Have a student-of-the-week or month award for the student who exhibits the finest character. Point out the student's patience, politeness, honesty, integrity, etc. You could involve the students in this by occasionally having a vote.

Encourage interest in world affairs.

115

Locate pen pals around the world for your students. Let them share or read the letters they receive to the class.

Create projects which will promote the acceptance of differences.

116

Consider having students sign their autographs.
Then make thumbprints of each student to pin
beside their autographs on a bulletin board.
Discuss the uniqueness of each individual.

Include small children in the decoration of their classroom.

117

Consider using the ancestral heritage from their
families, including family pictures,
coats of arms, family mottos,
and favorite family recipes.

118

Students need to know you have faith in them.

Express it. Predict success.

Problem-solving skills should be part of every curriculum.

119

Vary the topic. Teach students how to solve problems with friends, parents, teachers, and difficult people, who directly relate to their lives.

Make learning applicable to students' lives, while including as many of the five senses as possible.

120

For example: Perhaps they could paint a still life of vegetables before making a tossed salad! Point out how each food color represents a different classification of vitamins and minerals. Then, let them eat!

It's never too late to teach students how to organize themselves and their day.

Let your students make their own schedules. Encourage them each morning to plan their day, as well as record homework assignments and extra curricular activities.

122

Integrate your students' favorite pastimes into their studies.

During study hall, play contemporary
instrumental music softly in the background.

Don't overfunction for your students.

123

Be certain your students are doing their own work and that you are not being charmed into doing it for them!

124

An important skill for
students to learn is
how to arrange,
sort, categorize and
prioritize.

Show students how to order study information in
a notebook with a place for personalized notes,
handouts, assignments, and tests.

Critical-thinking skills are important for students to develop.

Train your students in critical thinking by assigning them the task of writing a summary of each of their days for 21 days, including what happened, what was good, what was unpleasant, and why.

Training in observation makes a more well-rounded student.

126

Send them out on a "journalistic" assignment in the school cafeteria. Have them write a paragraph of what they saw, heard, touched, felt, or tasted over lunch.

Help your students develop good study habits.

127

Instead of telling your older students to just
read a chapter, have them type out or write
its main points for extra credit. Encourage
them to use these notes as study tools
for their next test.

Grading systems should reward, not punish.

128

Develop a grading system which rewards
effort and extra energy put toward
school and academic activities.

Students appreciate the teacher keeping them advised as to what they can expect.

129

Keep students informed from
the beginning of the semester with
topics and issues you will be discussing with their
parents during parent-teacher conferences.

130

Genuine concern goes a long way toward keeping parents happy.

Periodically, pick up the phone and call parents
to tell them how their child is doing.

Immediately inform parents of a child's surfacing symptoms, *before* they turn into problems.

131

Help the parents to form a plan of action, set short-term goals, and discuss means for evaluating progress.

Always cool off before speaking out.

🍎 • 🍎 • 🍎

132

Emotional composure must be modeled if students are to grasp how to do it themselves.

The most effective way of gaining respect from students, is to treat them with respect.

133

Make an honest attempt to understand the ideas and feelings of your students. Always demonstrate your appreciation for the effort made, as well as the result. Affirm their right to hold a view different from yours. This may be the first time they experience this.

Use catchy rhymes, songs and phrases to reinforce important lessons.

134

Information that comes in the form of fun is more likely to stick with your students. This is a powerful memory technique. To test this, just ask them to sing or repeat a line from some of their favorite commercials!

Supervisors need to be informed, even when you are not certain the situation warrants it.

135

When in doubt, notify the Principal that they may be getting a phone call and why. It's always better to be informed than caught off guard.

Be resourceful.

136

You don't have to spend money to have a
treasury of inspirational tools available for
your students. Libraries have music, books on
tape, videos, framed art and a multitude of
items which can be checked out!

Create great expectations for your students.

137

Students have a way of rising to that higher standard, if they are empowered to do so and are aware of your belief in them. Showing them where they came from, the progress they've made, and how close they are to the goal — can be very inspirational to them.

Extend mercy and compassion toward students whenever possible.

We all make mistakes. Children learn certain lessons only through experience. Fortunately, most blunders can be corrected. Forgiveness of an innocent mistake, when rebuke was expected, could earn you the lifetime loyalty and devotion of that student.

Build a personal portfolio.

A portfolio can serve as a resumé to be shown to a prospective employer, or to simply chart your accomplishments. Include your awards and achievements, pictures and handouts of successful events or programs, stats on volunteer work, slides, audio cassettes, computer disks, sample work, etc.

139

Surveys show the average teen puts in 34.5 hours per week — *in after school activities alone!*

At the beginning of the year, help parents help their teens by setting priorities so they can avoid the trap of overcommitment.

Kids live in an interactive world.

141

Keep up with the times. Keep students' interest
by integrating television, video, films, and,
if possible, the computer and internet
into your daily lessons.

Structure healthy competition.

142

Allow each student to experience the
exhilaration of winning. Board games — chess,
for example, can develop both a healthy sense
of competition as well as strong
critical-thinking skills.

Encourage your students to get involved.

143

Studies show that students who get involved in extracurricular activities at school earn higher grades than those who are not involved.

Establish firm limits up front.

144

The first few days of the semester will set the tone for the entire semester. Relax later, *after* the students are clear about your expectations.

Teach the art of appreciation.

145

Toward the end of the semester, have each student write a brief note of appreciation to the classmate sitting near them.

Foster a spirit of thanksgiving within your students.

146

During Thanksgiving week, create a "thankful" box.
Have students anonymously write down the things they
are thankful for and drop their notes into the box.
The day before Thanksgiving vacation, students draw
from the box and read aloud the words of thankfulness
they created.

Help students learn to enjoy solitude rather than fear it.

147

Have students choose their favorite activities: reading, writing, or art. Each day allow a block of time for students to work on the activities they most enjoy — *by themselves*. Provide a quiet, peaceful environment for it.

Teach your students how to express themselves.

● · ● · ●

148

After reading a story, have the students
play charades and act out their favorite
character or part.

Keep the classroom environment alive!

Let your students plant seeds, grow plants, have an aquarium, pet bird, or even a gerbil! Have your students rotate turns taking care of them.

149

Get rid of the clutter!

150   Once, twice or three times each school year, have a spring cleaning session in your classroom. Have the students participate by helping you, as well as having them purge their own notebooks, lockers, desks and storage areas.

You cannot effectively lead others until you can manage yourself.

151

If you are not prepared, your students *will* know. Have a couple of back-up plans stashed away for a rainy day. You will be glad you did!

Good communication skills are essential to good parent-teacher relations.

152

Refrain from putting parents on the defensive. Be positive and constructive at all times and complimentary whenever possible.

Integrate writing into as many assignments as possible.

153

Having students use daily journals is an excellent way to help them overcome their fear of writing. They can chart their favorite things, the funniest thing that ever happened to them, their most embarrassing moment, etc.

Instill persistence in your students!

154

You can help your students stick it out by, breaking the tasks down into "baby-steps," talking them through their fears if they are intimidated, allotting more time, and cheering them on!

Celebrate with your students on the last week of school.

155

Tie a "Welcome Summer" sign on your class door, buy a
new pair of sunglasses, have snacks on your desk,
hold a class out on the school lawn under a tree, hand
out notes to each of your students letting them know
the gifts you see in them or have your students list the
things they most enjoyed about your class this year.

About the Author: Homer J. Adams

Dr. Homer Adams earned a Master's Degree from George Peabody College in Nashville, Tennessee, and later returned to earn his Doctor of Philosophy degree in History and Education at the same school. He has forty-three years experience as a high school social studies teacher, a history professor in college and university levels, and as dean and president in public and private colleges.

His achievements include Executive Dean at Dekalb and President of Trevecca Nazarene College, Nashville. He is the author of *Reminiscences of Dr. A. B. Mackey*, Trevecca Press, Nashville, Tennessee 1997. Today, Dr. Adams enjoys working as a freelance writer, part-time college professor, and speaker.